Read-About® Geography

Living in the Mountains

By Allan Fowler

Consultant
Linda Cornwell, Coordinator of School Quality
and Professional Improvement,
Indiana State Teachers Association

ℂℙ Children's Press®
A Division of Grolier Publishing
New York   London   Hong Kong   Sydney
Danbury, Connecticut

Visit Children's Press® on the Internet at:
http://publishing.grolier.com

Designer: Herman Adler Design Group

Library of Congress Cataloging-in-Publication Data

Fowler, Allan.
    Living in the mountains / by Allan Fowler; consultant, Linda Cornwell.
      p. cm. — (Rookie read-about geography)
    ISBN: 0-516-21563-9 (lib. bdg.)   0-516-27051-6 (pbk.)
    1. Mountains Juvenile literature. 2. Mountain people Juvenile
literature. 3. Human geography Juvenile literature. 4. Mountain
ecology Juvenile literature. [1. Mountains. 2. Human geography.
3. Mountain ecology. 4. Ecology.] I. Title. II. Series.
GF57.F68   2000
910`.02143—dc21   99-30441
                                           CIP

GROLIER
PUBLISHING   1 2 3 4 5 6 7 8 9 10 R 09 08 07 06 05 04 03 02 01 00

Many people live in areas where there are mountains.

People who live in
mountain areas may make
their homes in a valley.

A valley is a long, low
place between hills or
mountains.

Beaver Creek, Colorado, is a valley town.

Mountains rising from a plateau

Some mountains rise from a plateau (pla-TOH). A plateau is land that is high and mostly flat. Cities, towns, and farmlands can be found on plateaus.

The city of Denver, Colorado, sits on a plateau. The people there enjoy views of the Rocky Mountains.

Denver, Colorado

Many other cities are located in the mountain areas of the United States. They include: Albuquerque (AL-buh-ker-kee), New Mexico, and Salt Lake City, Utah.

WASHINGTON

MONTANA

NORTH DAKOTA

MINNESOTA

R O C K Y   M O U N T A I N S

OREGON

IDAHO

WYOMING

SOUTH DAKOTA

WISCONSIN

MICHIGAN

NEW HAMPSHIRE

VERMONT

MAINE

NEBRASKA

IOWA

NEW YORK

Massachusetts

NEVADA

Salt Lake City

UTAH

COLORADO

Denver

KANSAS

MISSOURI

ILLLINOIS

INDIANA

OHIO

PENNSYLVANIA

WEST VIRGINIA

Rhode Island

Connecticut

New Jersey

CALIFORNIA

UNITED STATES

KENTUCKY

VIRGINIA

Delaware

Maryland

OKLAHOMA

TENNESSEE

NORTH CAROLINA

ARIZONA

Albuquerque

NEW MEXICO

ARKANSAS

ALABAMA

SOUTH CAROLINA

A P P A L A C H I A N   M O U N T A I N S

TEXAS

MISSISSIPPI

GEORGIA

LOUISIANA

FLORIDA

North

West   East

South

Coal miners in the Appalachian Mountains

Mountains are often rich in minerals, such as iron or copper.

The Appalachian (a-puh-LAY-shun) Mountains are located in the eastern United States. Many towns there began near coal mines. Today, many people in Appalachia make a living as coal miners.

Islands are really mountains that have risen from the ocean floor.

Their tops peak above the water.

15

Japan is a country made up of islands. Japan doesn't have much flat land for farms. So the people grow their food in the sides of hills.

Vegetables growing in the hillsides of Japan

Volcano crater

Some mountains have an opening called a crater. This type of mountain is called a volcano.

Deep beneath the volcano is hot, melted rock called lava. Sometimes the lava flows out of the volcano.

The state of Hawaii is made up of islands. They are the tops of volcanoes that rose from deep beneath the ocean.

One of the Hawaiian Islands

Pineapple farmworker

22

Some Hawaiians work on farms and in industries on the islands. Pineapple farms are found all over Hawaii.

Other Hawaiians work with people who visit Hawaii on vacation.

24

The world's tallest mountains are found in Tibet. Tibet is part of China. Its mountains are called the Himalaya.

Many Tibetans live
on plateaus where the
land is good for farming.
Some Tibetans raise yaks.
Yaks are oxen with long,
shaggy hair.

Tibetan farmers use yaks to plow fields.

Mountain areas can be great places to live. Some people who don't live near mountains like to visit them to go hiking, camping, fishing, or skiing.

Words You Know

Denver, Colorado

Hawaii

Himalaya Mountains

Japan

miners

plateau

valley

volcano

yaks

Index

About the Author

Allan Fowler is a freelance writer with a background in advertising. Born in New York, he now lives in Chicago and enjoys traveling.

Photo Credits

©: International Stock Photo: 17, 31 top left (Chad Ehlers); Landslides Aerial Photography: 21, 30 top right (Alex S. MacLean); Liaison Agency Inc.: 3 (Roy Gumpel), 22 (Ed Lallo), 18, 31 bottom left (G. Brad Lewis), 29 (Aaron Strong); Peter Arnold Inc.: 27, 31 bottom right (Malcolm S. Kirk), 9, 30 top left (Alex S. MacLean), 5, 31 center right (Jim Wark); Photo Researchers: 12, 31 top right (RAPHO); Robert Fried Photography: 24, 30 bottom; The Image Works: 6, 31 center left (N. Richmond); Tony Stone Images: cover (Manfred Mehlig), 15 (A & L Sinibaldi).

Map by Joe LeMonnier.